T0201780

The BOWING of the STARS

Patience, Trust, and Forgiveness from Surah Yusuf,
the Qur'an's 'Best of Stories'

Mehded Maryam Sinclair

Art and Design by MforMoon İllustration
Calligraphy by Na'ecl Cajee

In the Name of Allah, Most Merciful and Compassionate
All Praise to Allah, Mighty and Majestic, the Lord of the Worlds, and to His Messenger
Muhammad, may Allah bless him and give him peace.

The Bowing of the Stars
Patience, Trust, and Forgiveness from Surah Yusuf,
the Qur'an's 'Best of Stories'

First Published in 2024 by THE ISLAMIC FOUNDATION

Distributed by
KUBE PUBLISHING LTD
MCC, Ratby Lane, Markfield, Leicestershire, UK Tel: +44 (0) 1530 249230
E-Mail: info@kubepublishing.com Website: www.kubepublishing.com

Author: Mehded Maryam Sinclair

Illustrator and design: MforMoon

A Cataloguing-in-Publication Data record for this book is available from the
British Library.

ISBN Hardback 978-0-86037-924-9

ISBN Ebook 978-0-86037-929-4

Printed in Turkey

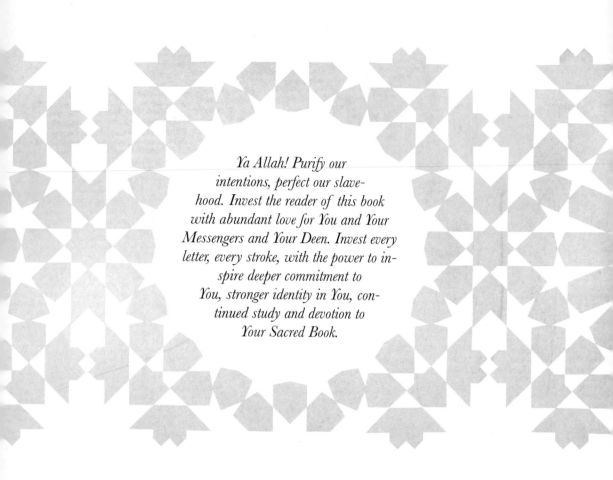

Ya Allah! Purify our intentions, perfect our slave-hood. Invest the reader of this book with abundant love for You and Your Messengers and Your Deen. Invest every letter, every stroke, with the power to in-spire deeper commitment to You, stronger identity in You, con-tinued study and devotion to Your Sacred Book.

DEDICATIONS

For Sheikh Ali Hani, who has fathomed the infinite seas of Qur'an for the treasures like those you will find in this book. May deeper searching, dear reader, be the joy of your life.

In memory of the late Sheikh Nuh Ali Salman al Qudah, the former Grand Mufti of the Hashemite Kingdom of Jordan, may Allah be pleased with him.

TABLE OF CONTENTS

FOREWORD

The way of the Qur'anic narrative is to mention the most important details that relate to the primary lessons that are being taught in any Qur'anic story, and the rest of the details are left out; left for the reader to imagine the events that might have transpired in between the lines, an imagination that is aided by context, common sense and the many hints subtly pointing to them in the Qur'an. For one to fill in these gaps and contemplate on them is part of interacting with Qur'anic stories. In fact, there are times when such interaction is essential to fully understand the lessons that are to be learnt.

The following story of the life of Prophet Yusuf, may the peace and blessings of Allah be upon him, follows the Qur'anic narrative style. The story is completely in accordance with the Qur'anic account with details filled in from the author's very able imagination. All extra details are completely in accordance with the spirit and soul of the story. They help one piece together the events and are especially useful for children to really appreciate the wonder and miracle of the story, as well as to recognise that these are real events. None of the details contradict any Islamic values and many can be found in the copious literature of Qur'anic interpretation.

I have checked the story for accuracy, relying on the following great works in Qur'anic interpretation:

Irshad al 'Aql al Salim by Abu al Su'ud
Ruh al Ma'ani by al Alusi
al Tahrir wa al Tanwir by Ibn 'Ashur
Nadhm al Durar by al Biqa'i
Sura Yusuf by Ahmad Nawfal

I believe this present work to be an excellent contribution to much-needed literature that invites the reader to truly absorb and enter the world of the Qur'an. The beautiful writing style of the author corresponds nicely to the magical and compelling style of the Qur'anic original.

And Allah alone gives success.

Sheikh Ali Hani
17th June 2008
Amman, Jordan

INTRODUCTION

The tale you are about to encounter is one of the world's oldest and most beloved stories. It was recited to the Best of Creation, Muhammad, may Allah bless him and give him peace, as a comfort to him during his Year of Sadness, at the very time when his enemies were trying to prove that he was ignorant. It was recited to him in the best of languages, Arabic, by the best of the angels, Jibril, may Allah be pleased with him, at the best of places, near the Kaaba.

It is the most beautiful of stories because it gives us what we most need. It shows us what happens to those who have faith, sincerity, patience, good character, and optimism. It also shows us, to the contrary, what people are like when they think only of themselves, when they listen to the whisperings of Shaytan and when they are convinced that this world is all there is.

This is not a translation of what Jibril, peace upon him, brought from Allah, nor what Muhammad, may Allah bless him and give him peace, received from him, nor yet what his companions and followers down to this present day have memorised and recited. But it follows the Revelation in every detail, and does not contradict it in any way. I pray that it will cause your love for the Qur'an to deepen, intensify your desire for its pristine clarity, and draw you into the depths of its majesty.

The critical point to understand is that these events narrated here truly happened. As Allah Mighty and Majestic tells us, it is NOT just a 'tale of the ancients'. This means there was indeed a well, and very likely snakes lived in or around it - that is what we know about wells. The idea that a snake might lose the power of its poison for bothering one of Allah's beloveds does not distort anything we know of physical reality. There is nothing in all we have been told about Paradise that would prevent the possibility of a white rose garden there.

The Prophet Yusuf did walk this earth, was betrayed by brothers and then by his slave-owner's wife, and then was imprisoned for long years while his father wept for him, never once giving up hope of being reunited with him.

And once the events had happened, the astonished humans, who saw, heard, tasted, smelled and touched them, told them and retold them, over and over, down through generations. They re-lived them with every telling, because that is what humans do. Whatever happens to them, whatever they experience, they tell, have you noticed? And, as always happens with hear-say, as these events got told over and over they got a little mixed up. Things got forgotten, or exaggerated, or changed.

Alhamdulillah, we possess the unwavering certainty of the Qur'anic Revelation. Jibril, peace upon him, was sent by Allah Mighty and Majestic to narrate the truth of all things, subhanAllah. This certainty allows us to discern and evaluate the various early oral accounts and retellings that have arisen, including those that have been claimed to be Revelation.

Guidance from esteemed scholars, such as Jordan's former Grand Mufti Nuh Ali Salman al Qudah, may Allah be pleased with him, and Pakistan's Mufti Taqi Usmani, suggests that we may draw upon details from these traditional narratives or point out other possible details that, according to the Qur'anic narrative, would be expected to have existed in the full-blown physical reality of the event. This is permissible as long as these details are within the parameters set by the Qur'an, and do not undermine its indisputable meanings in any way.

This approach, inshaAllah, can serve as a means to open hearts and captivate imaginations for His sake. With a loving heart, inshaAllah, you will find yourself returning repeatedly to the ocean that is Qur'an to reflect on what Allah has told us, and how He has done so.

I would like to acknowledge the extraordinary efforts of Jordanian tafsir scholar Sheikh Ali Hani, and his student and translator Sheikh Sohail Hanif, for the hours upon hours of time they spent examining and refining every sentence of this work.

TABLE OF CALLIGRAPHY

CANAA...

EGYPT

Nile River

N
W   E
S

CHAPTER ONE
Into the Well

The young shepherd Yusuf woke up with his father, long before everyone else, and went out with him, out under the overarching sky still glittering with stars. Cold water shivered over his smooth olive skin and made his black hair stand on end. His eyes delighted in the dark shapes of the hills and distant peaks, of near and far-flung olive trees, upon a vast flatness that rolled out in every direction to meet the sky.

His forty goats clambered and crowded around him, interested in the splashing water, trying to get their share. His father, Yaqub, peace upon him, sat on a grass mat on the sand with his head bowed, praying in gratitude to the One God, Who is continually creating all that exists in the heavens and the earth.

Yaqub had learned this prayer from his father Ishaq, peace upon him, and Ishaq had learned it from his own father, Ibrahim, peace upon him. They were like jewelled beads, strung on the same gold chain, running down through time.

Yusuf sat down beside him and listened to the silence, and in that silence it seemed to him that everything he saw was singing a song of gratitude, just like his father was. Sometimes it even seemed to him that he could hear Ishaq's and Ibrahim's prayers too, from the Unseen. Some of the sounds he could hear with his ears, like the goats' songs, or the wind rustling the tent-flaps, or the chorus of dawn birds. The other sounds, the voices of the rocks, of the sand, of the still air, of the water in the water-jars, the ones no one could hear, Yusuf heard in his heart, and they were as real to him as all the others, and gave him a pleasure almost too large to hold.

When Yaqub got up, Yusuf helped him bring manure bricks to kindle the morning fire. A new light was just beginning to open in the east now, and on the dark side of the sky a few stars glimmered bravely on.

He held a long piece of straw into the fire. "*Abati*, I saw a strange dream."

Yaqub, peace upon him, looked at him. "Did you now? Well, tell it to me"

"In the name of Allah I will tell it to you...in the night sky, I saw eleven bright stars and the sun and

يَا أَبَتِ

the moon."

Yaqub leaned closer. "Beautiful, Yusuf. Go on. What happened then?"

"*Abati*, the eleven stars bowed before me. And the sun and the moon bowed before me."

The first rays of rising sun shot across the land and the brilliant blue desert flowers quivered.

Yusuf noticed that the birds had suddenly stopped their singing. Yaqub was very still, and Yusuf could hear him whispering a prayer.

"Look, my son. You mustn't say a thing about this to your brothers. It's a very important dream you've had, and they won't be able to understand it. If they get the wrong idea, the Shaytan might get them to try to hurt you. Jealousy makes people do strange things sometimes."

The olive branches groaned in the wind.

"But *Abati*, what does it mean?"

"You have been chosen to carry the secrets, Yusuf. You will be one of those who can see the meanings behind everything that happens. The vision and wisdom that was Allah's gift to your grandfather Ishaq and your great-grandfather Ibrahim will be yours to carry. Because you will be one who shows the way, a prophet, we will all honor you, all your brothers, your mother…"

Yaqub held his son close, and caressed his head. "Do you know something, Yusuf? I waited ninety-one years for you to come. When I married your mother, Rachel, I knew something wonderful was going to happen. When you were still inside your mother's womb I knew you had finally come to us. I have been expecting this dream!"

Yusuf and Yaqub had never been far away from each other. But after that day, they were even closer. Perhaps Yusuf peeled his fruit for him, or rubbed his feet. He might have sung songs to him. Sometimes they might walk far off together, to listen to the silence. They never tried to exclude anyone. But really, nobody ever wanted to go with them, except for Yusuf's younger brother, Binyamin, and he was too young.

Yusuf had ten half brothers and one younger full brother, Binyamin, born, as he himself had been, to Rachel. The older ones had no news of the secrets, no news of the Unseen, and so they were jealous. Their jealousy grew long and black in their hearts. They watched one night as Yaqub and Yusuf walked out across the wide dunes to watch the star-dazzled sky.

"Look at them! They're always together," said Judah.

"He doesn't even look at us anymore. Ten fine, strong, bold sons he has but he doesn't even remember us." Rubin said, scowling.

"*Abana* hardly ever goes off by himself to walk anymore, either," Judah snarled. "Have you noticed? He's always busy with Yusuf." He flung a stone out into the darkness. "I hate Yusuf! I wish we could just get rid of him. What if we just kill him, or at least drag him away from here so we won't have to see him anymore!"

"Look, Judah, we can't kill Yusuf, our own brother." He kicked up the sand with his sandal. "But … we can see to it that he gets lost."

Judah's jaw dropped. "Lost?"

"Lost?" the other boys echoed.

"Yes. Lost." Rubin stood up and leaned against the olive tree. "I know an old, deep, dark, terrible well. They say it has no bottom. It is way out on the desert highway. We'll drop him into it. If he lives through it, the next caravan to pass through will find him, help him out, and take him far away from here."

"What a brilliant plan, Rubin. Let's do it!"

"Not so fast, Judah. We'll have to convince *Abana* to give us permission first." Rubin got up and plucked a branch of olive leaves and flung it out across the sand. "We'll say we want to take him on a little outing. Let's sleep on it and figure it out tomorrow."

A few days later when Rubin and Judah were filling water jugs with Yaqub, peace upon him, Rubin asked, "*Abana*, why is it you do not ever trust us with Yusuf? He is getting older now…."

"Yes, *Abana*," Judah said. Let Yusuf come with us tomorrow. We only want what's best for him. We will guard him perfectly."

Yaqub, peace upon him, felt an ache in the pit of his stomach. "Yusuf is too young. It would grieve me to let him go. You will all be busy with your own affairs. You'll go off and leave him alone and he'll find trouble. There are …there are wolves…"

If you had asked the stone water-jars, they would have reminded you of the old saying: *Calamity depends upon the word that comes out of the mouth.* Yaqub, peace upon him, had said what he feared…

He stopped and put down his water-jar. His hands were shaking. He took a small white cloth from the folds of his robe and wiped his face with it.

"*Abana*," Rubin said. "We won't forget him, we won't leave him, even for an instant."

"And anyway, we are ten strong brothers," said Judah. "If a wolf came near us, he would have to eat his way through all of us to get to Yusuf!"

Rubin set down his heavy jug for a moment. "Let him come with us, *Abana*. We'll bring him right back. He really wants to come. He will be very disappointed if you say no."

Yaqub, peace upon him, felt the knot in his stomach tighten. There seemed to be nothing more to say. He gave his permission.

They picked up their water jugs and hurried to the tents. They made their plans, gathered their supplies, and early the next morning they were ready to go. Yusuf was wearing his favourite tunic of blues and greens. Yaqub saw how excited the boy was about going with his big brothers. He felt a little easier, but the knot of fear in his stomach was still there.

"Remember your promises to me, Rubin, and don't let him out of your sight."

"I will remember, and I won't take my eyes off him, *Abana*, Don't worry about a thing." Nobody noticed the dark glance he gave to Judah as he finished talking.

As long as they were within sight of Yaqub, Rubin kept his arm around Yusuf's shoulders. But as soon as they were out of sight, he dropped his arm and pushed his brother away. They walked along, faster now, in the direction of the desert highway. When they stopped, they all stood around him.

"So, Yusuf," smirked Simeon. "You're a big boy now, right? You don't have your *aba* fawning over everything you do, for once?"

Rubin tousled Yusuf's hair and pulled his ear. "Yusuf, we found a little adventure you might like, on this first trip away from your *aba*."

Yusuf turned away from Simeon. But then Judah and Levi stepped forward. They pulled his hair and slapped his face and ears. They were all laughing now. Yusuf began to fight back, but how could he fight off ten big brothers?

Yusuf began to struggle. "Rubin, please. Help me."

Rubin grabbed Judah by the shoulders and pushed him aside. "You don't have to beat him up. I told you, we'll throw him in the well."

"Right. Let's do it and get it over with," Judah said. "I'm sick of looking at him!"

They dragged him

kicking and screaming to the mouth of the well - nothing more than a pile of stones now. The centuries had worn it down. Time had worn away its beautiful exterior, as it wears away all exteriors.

"Wait!" cried Rubin. "Give me his shirt."

They ripped his shirt from him. They tied his hands behind his back. Rubin grabbed his right shoulder, Judah the left, and Simeon seized his feet, and they heaved him into the depths of darkness, down, down, down.

The time of his falling was only a few seconds. But in that time, it is said, a message came for Jibril, who was in heaven's white rose garden. The message was, "Help Yusuf, the son of Yaqub, the grandson of Ibrahim." They say Jibril flew immediately to the well. He caught Yusuf in the middle of his fall, and set him down gently on a rock ledge near the bottom of the well. The ropes fell away from his wrists. He stood alone on the rock, trembling, and then a voice sounded in his heart.

"Yusuf, remember Us. We will not desert you. You cannot understand now, but it will all become clear in the end. And you will one day tell your brothers about what they are doing to you, at a time when they do not know who you are."

Another old tale tells how the walls of the well were full of little nooks and crannies where poisonous spiders and lizards and snakes lived.

"Be still. Don't move, don't make a sound, don't be seen, because today a prophet, one who shows the way, has come down into our well as a trial to make him strong."

But there was one rebellious snake that did not listen to the other creatures. He began slithering toward Yusuf. His jaws were wide open. His poisonous tongue was darting. A terrible chattering sound came from him. Yusuf felt all the hair stand up on the back of his neck. Little drops of sweat poured from his face.

Jibril said, "Be silent. Go away."

The snake stopped suddenly. Its head dropped, its jaw snapped shut, and not a sound came from it. It turned and slithered away. And from that day on, the tale tells us, all the descendants of that snake are silent, and have lost the power of their poison.

Yusuf had grown up at his father's knees, learning the religion of his ancestors, Prophets Adam, Nuh, Salih, Hud, Lut, Ibrahim, peace upon them one and all. A dua sprang into his heart and rolled effortlessly off his tongue.

Down there in the darkness, he might have sat on the stone and said the prayer again and again. With each repetition, he would have felt stronger. He'd have felt his fear vanish, and in its place, patience would have brought the dawn to his heart.

His prayer would have been so fervent that even the other angels would have heard it and wanted to come close, surrounding him with their unseen wings.

*O Allah, the One Who
answers every prayer, the One
Who lifts all burdens, Who eases all
pains, the One Who is the Companion to
those Who feel alone. There is no one but
You, there is no one equal to You, there is no
rest except with You, no peace except with
You. Please make my heart full of Your
love, so full that fear has no place, so
full that I will not remember anything except You, O Allah.*

His brothers left the well laughing and slapping each other on the back. On the way home, they caught and killed a little goat and stained Yusuf's shirt with its blood. It was long past sundown by the time they reached their little circle of goat-hair tents, and they had changed their laughter to fake tears and false sobbing.

When they entered their father's dark tent, he stirred on his reed mat and sat up.

"What is it? Have you lost one of your sheep?"

When he saw Yusuf was not with them, his heart missed a beat. He stood up. "Where is Yusuf?"

The brothers cried harder.

"O *Abana!*" said Rubin. "We were racing each other. Yusuf was sitting with our packs. Then suddenly we looked…. a wolf had devoured every scrap of him."

Judah said, "We couldn't help him, *Abana*. It was too late."

Yaqub went pale. When he saw the bloodied greens and blues of Yusuf's favourite tunic he felt hollow inside. He took it from them and looked at it carefully. He held the shirt to his face and wept.

"You are trapped in the web of your own tales. You have made something horrible seem good to you…and what about me?"

"*Abana*!" Judah cried. "You never believe us! Even if we were telling the truth, you would never believe us."

"For me the only truth, my son, the only trustworthy one, is my Maker, the Lord of the Unseen. I hope I may have endless perfect patience, and have no complaint except to Allah, and no hopelessness, and wait for His Mercy."

For days Yaqub stayed alone and did not speak a word to anyone. His eyes grew red from weeping, and the shirt became soaked not only with false blood but with tears.

Some say Yusuf stayed three days in the well. Others say it was only a few hours. But who can measure such things? He stayed as long as it took for the work of the Unseen to be accomplished, as long as it takes for the apple to turn from green to red on the tree. Or maybe it was as long as it takes for bread to rise in the pan, or as long as it takes for the snows to melt and the fish to swim upstream.

On another day, just after sunset, a caravan stopped at the well for water. The thirsty water-bearer lowered his pail down into the well. Suddenly he heard Yusuf's cries. "Hey!" he said. "There's a boy down there."

"Help! Help me!" Yusuf cried. "Pull me out of here."

"Wait! I'll bring a stronger rope." The water-bearer dashed off to his camel and pulled an enormous rope out of a sack. He called to three other travellers who had just arrived.

"Come here! There's somebody down in the well. We'll have to pull him out."

"Look at him," one traveller said as Yusuf kicked and scrambled his way out. "He's a fine, strong youth. Where did he come from, I wonder?"

"He must be a slave," said another, "or else he'd be with his family and not hiding in the bottom of a well."

"We'll get a fortune for him if we sell him, that's for sure. Let's hide him and take him with us."

CHAPTER TWO
The Slave of the Aziz

Bound hand and foot to a camel, Yusuf repeated the prayer we imagined he'd learned as a child. As his tongue recited, whenever his thoughts drifted to worry and fear, he dragged them back again, to his eyes - the hills and rocks, the swirling sands and stubbly trees, the vast open sky and rolling clouds. Or to his nose - the smell of the camel, the sweetness of the breeze, the occasional scent of desert sage. Or to his ears - the creaking of the saddle, the snorting of the camel, the cry of the hawk overhead. The easiest times were the nights, under the stars, when the guidance he'd received from his father Yaqub, peace upon him, the guidance in the remembrance of the Creator, stilled and expanded his heart so there was no room for worry or fear.

Gradually they left the deserted by-ways and found themselves among people and their pack-animals bustling along narrowing windy roads. Soon they had come into the centre of the thronging city and all around them rose a cacophony of men's and women's voices calling out their wares for sale, donkeys braying, dogs barking, children calling out, great carts groaning along laden with clucking hens and crowing roosters, small herds of sheep and goats bleating their way to the meat-knife.

Then they came to a stop, right in the middle of the slave market. All around were small groups of slaves, tied hand to hand in dirty white robes or nothing at all, some sitting or lying on the ground, some standing to endure the inspection of a would-be master. There were men and boys. There were women, some with babies tied to their backs or nursing at their breasts.

They untied Yusuf roughly and threw him to the ground. He struggled to his feet and within moments was surrounded by a clutch of men eager to find out more about him. They could see what a fine lad he was, handsome, strong, quick-witted, intelligent. They thought he was beautiful and they tried to outbid each other until finally he was sold to an official of the king of the land. And so the price was paid, and Yusuf was sold as a slave.

The finest, the purest, the brother, the favourite son, was sold for a pitiful handful of silver.

Allah Mighty and Majestic related the story to Muhammad, may Allah bless him and give him peace, through the Angel Jibril, peace upon him, saying, "Thus did We establish Yusuf in the land of Egypt." Yusuf's brothers intended to humiliate him at the bottom of the well, but Allah elevated him. The traders wanted to sell him as a slave, but in the end…well, read on, and you shall hear. Allah says "Be!" and it is.

When the Aziz, the official of the king, took his new slave home, he took him right into his own home to his wife Zulaykha, instead of to the slave-quarters.

"Zulaykha, he will stay here with us. We must care for him well. Maybe we can adopt him as our son, or at least maybe some good will come to us from him. For he is a rare treasure of a young man; see how patiently he does what he is told."

And so Yusuf became a house-slave in the home of the Aziz.

Zulaykha was a beautiful woman. And she was an honourable woman. She patiently taught Yusuf all his household duties and saw to his needs, and as the days passed, then the weeks, then the months, then the years, he grew into a sturdy tree of a man.

And then one day she noticed all at once how his face had become the face of a man, the man, you will remember, to whom Allah Mighty and Majestic had given half of all the beauty of humankind. In an instant her life changed. She said nothing. She put down the basket of rose petals she'd been holding. She went to her own room. She sat without moving for hours.

The next day, she worked not to pay attention to his face, to his strong hands and arms, to his noble manner. But when she was alone, every time she closed her eyes, it was his image she'd see, his voice she'd hear, the way he'd spoken so kindly to the goatherd, the incredible light and compassion of his smile as he greeted the carpenter's children, the patience and forbearance with which he responded to the carelessness of the orchard-keeper.

From that day on, her servants all began noticing a change in her.

"Has the evil eye struck her?" asked one.

"Or is it the demons?" asked another.

"No," said a third. "I think she must be in love, but with whom?"

But when Zulaykha came into the room, they fell silent. "The wax is dripping onto the floor," Zulaykha said vacantly. What she was really saying, inside herself where no one but Allah could hear, was, "I am longing to see Yusuf."

Later, she said, "Look, the moon is up." But what she really meant was, "Yusuf is beautiful, like the moon."

Every day, many times a day, she would say something like, "The roses are fragrant," or "The coriander seeds are roasting," or "The water is cool and fresh," but what she was really saying was, "I saw Yusuf today."

If she said, "There is no breeze," or "My head hurts," or "I am so tired," what she was really saying was, "I miss Yusuf. Where is he?"

Each day she lived, she lived for him. She waited to see him in the mornings, and if, by the end of the day she had not seen him, the night was long and dark and friendless. She started arranging her day around him, so that she could be near him as much as possible.

One day she waited for him in the sitting room at the edge of the garden. She expected that he would come in through the garden door, since he was busy with the grape harvest and was preparing the drying racks. She locked the other doors to the room, and after he came in and was busy laying the grapes out on the racks, she quickly locked the door he'd just used. She went up behind him, trembling to be so close to him.

"Dear Yusuf, you work so hard. Come, sit with me for a moment."

Yusuf whirled around, alarmed by the sweetness of her voice. When he saw the look in her eyes, his heart started to pound and the grapes he'd been holding fell to the floor.

"Yusuf, I have been watching you. Look. Do you see how I have dressed up to please you?"

"What?! I seek refuge in Allah! What are you doing, my Mistress? Words like that are for your husband, not for his slave."

"Your eyes are so beautiful…" She reached to hold his hand but he drew back suddenly as if something had burned him. She had always been so kind to him, taken such good care of him. He struggled to understand, but he could not. Something was terribly wrong.

"When I am dead in the ground my eyes will be the first to fall into the dirt," he said. "Your husband is more worthy of your beauty than anyone else. May Allah help me. I cannot be disloyal to my master, the Aziz, who has treated me so well. Wrongdoers never come to good, Zulaykha."

He turned and fled to the furthermost door and struggled to unlock it. She ran after him. "Wait! Please don't go." She grabbed his shirt and the fine cloth ripped. The door flew open and there stood the Aziz, just coming in.

"How shall you reward this slave of yours, my husband? What is the fitting punishment for one who has an evil intention towards your wife? Throw him into prison. Or find something worse!"

All the colour drained from the Aziz's face. A few of the household servants drew near, listening, watching. He looked at Yusuf, who looked straight back into his eyes, the look of an honest man with nothing to hide.

Other servants came when they heard the commotion.

The Aziz looked from Zulaykha to Yusuf, scarcely believing his ears. The silence was cut then by the voice of Zulaykha's own uncle.

"Well, if his shirt is torn from the front, then her story is true. But if it is torn from the back, then he is telling the truth and she is lying."

The Aziz saw that Yusuf's shirt was indeed torn from the back.

"So, Zulaykha, it is you who is lying! Yusuf…please…overlook this. Please pretend it never happened." The Aziz whirled toward Zulaykha, his chest heaving with rage.

"You have done a terrible thing, Zulayka. Get out of my sight. Go and seek forgiveness."

Zulaykha went to her room and slammed the door. Yusuf, shaken and sad, walked out across the stone courtyard and out under the grape vines. We can imagine how he might have appealed for help to his Master Allah Mighty and Majestic:

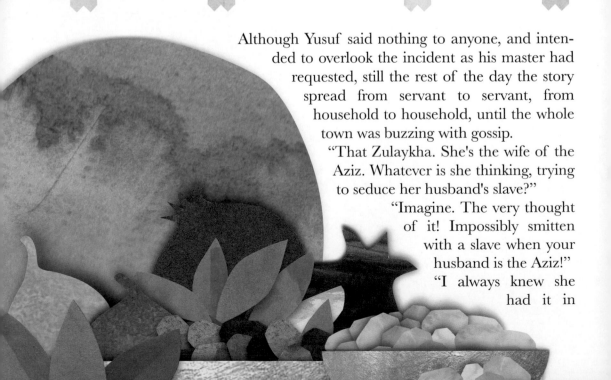

"My Lord!
I am so grateful to You! I
want nothing more than to stay
near You. Please, O please, protect
me from the pull of my passions, from
anything that will displease You and
separate me from knowing You in
every breath! Please release me
from myself!"

Although Yusuf said nothing to anyone, and intended to overlook the incident as his master had requested, still the rest of the day the story spread from servant to servant, from household to household, until the whole town was buzzing with gossip.

"That Zulaykha. She's the wife of the Aziz. Whatever is she thinking, trying to seduce her husband's slave?"

"Imagine. The very thought of it! Impossibly smitten with a slave when your husband is the Aziz!"

"I always knew she had it in

her to do something like this!"

"She's really sunk low this time."

The next day Zulaykha was brushing her hair. Her friend came into the room.

"I've just come from the fountain. Is there a single woman here who does not know about your 'adventure' yesterday, I wonder? My face was burning up by the time I could get away from them, and they weren't even talking about me."

"What are they saying?"

"Why, they are talking about what a dangerous woman you are."

Zulaykha put down her hairbrush and looked long at her face in the mirror.

"Dangerous? Hmm...We shall see."

She called a servant. "Please, tell the cook to roast the fattest geese and pick the best and freshest fruits he can find. Tell him to bake braided loaves and layered buns and sweet stuffed honey rolls. We'll invite the ladies to tea this afternoon."

She went downstairs. When she saw Yusuf, she acted as if nothing had happened. But if you had been close to her, you'd have heard her heart pounding and seen the blush on her cheeks.

"Yusuf! You will have work here this afternoon. See that you do not go far away."

The ladies sat together in the late afternoon sun on big purple and red cushions. In the middle was a low round table, covered with a brilliant gold cloth. Succulent roast geese nested saucily amid piles of crusty dark breads. Baskets sagged with crimson pomegranates and luscious figs, trays were piled high with halved and seeded pale green melons and dripping cantaloupes, and red and black and petite white grapes spilled over little plates. There were small bowls of raisins, deep bowls of date syrup, and wide saucers of creamy sesame paste. Glistening candied hibiscus blossoms rested on the rims of mugs of cool rosy tea sweetened with honey. Each woman received a plate and a small bone-handled knife, and the servants moved among them serving the delectable treats, all they could ever want.

The conversation was a bit restrained at first, as gossip always has a way of secretly dividing people without their ever being aware of it, but soon enough talk and

laughter became easy again as the guests enjoyed the feast.

Nobody noticed Zulaykha whisper to her servant, "Send for Yusuf. Tell him to come here for a moment, and make his entrance."

But when the long heavy curtain was drawn back a few moments later, when Yusuf walked into their midst, the room became silent in an instant. Next there came the sound of bloodied bone-handled knives falling onto the plates as each and every woman gashed her hand instead of her fruit in her utter astonishment.

"Zulaykha, who is this?"

"Surely this is no mortal man."

"He must have come from the Afterworld."

Zulaykha stood in front of the ladies. "My friends, this is the man about whom you accuse me. But now I ask you, all of you, what happened to you when you saw him? Or do you always carve into your hands when you are eating fruit? It's all true, everything you accuse me of. I did try to seduce him, and he resisted me." She wiped a tear from her eye. "How could I not fall for him, seeing him every day, being the receiver of his kindness and respect?"

Then she shook her head and thrust her chin in the air. Her golden medallion bounced at her throat. "But is he not, in fact, a slave? Is he not my slave, by virtue of his being my husband's slave? Now I say with all of you as my witness that I will have my way with him, since he is my slave, and if he continues to resist me, he will be thrown into prison, which is the fitting punishment for a disobedient slave. Yes, Yusuf, You may go now."

As he made his way out of the room, he heard the women around him calling out to him.

"O my God! In a roomful of women Zulaykha uttered the most awful promise. What can I do? Where can I run? O Allah! Turn their plot away from me, or I will be lost and become one of the ignorant! Better for me to be in prison than to have to face these women again and again!"

"Sweet Yusuf, just do as she asks. She will surely reward you."

Yusuf left the room immediately and ran to his own quarters. He was shaking. He fell to his knees.

Allah heard his prayer, and answered it at once.

The women, too, were shocked. They each went home to their husbands and related the story of Zulaykha's lustful intentions. Within a few days a group of men huddled around the Aziz.

"This is getting out of hand, Sir. We must do something, and soon."

"I trust Yusuf," said the Aziz, "and I know he is not contributing to this fire, but clearly he cannot stay here in my house just now. He must go to prison, or something even more unpleasant is bound to happen."

CHAPTER THREE
Imprisoned

"Yusuf! Open the door! You must come with us at once!"

The prison was not far, but it was dark, and it was cold, and it was damp.

Yusuf went with the guard without a struggle. As he climbed down the narrow clammy mud steps, we might imagine him remembering another place he'd been in long before, and the prayer he'd repeated over and over, deep down in the sun-forsaken well, the prayer that had brought dawn to his heart

O Allah, the One Who answers every prayer, the One Who lifts all burdens, Who eases all pains, the One Who is the Companion to those Who feel alone. There is no one but You, there is no one equal to You, there is no rest except with You, no peace except with You. Please make my heart full of Your love, so full that fear has no place, so full that I will not remember anything except You, O Allah

in the darkest of moments, fell effortlessly from his lips.

His countenance was so wide, so sweet, that the men felt ashamed to imprison him, and the prison guards wanted to do all they could to please him.

With the other prisoners, some foreigners, some palace servants, he worked from sun-up until sundown sorting grain and heaving sacks. He listened to every word a man said, and he listened too for the words that weren't said, the ones that couldn't be said. The others came to trust him and seek him out for his gift of listening, his kindness, his humble ways.

One of the prisoners had been the king's chief butler. He had come into prison around the same time as Yusuf. One morning early, before anyone else was awake, before the sun had risen, he came upon Yusuf on his knees. Yusuf did not see him, so the man coughed politely and waited. Another man came near. This man had also been a servant in the palace, the king's baker. He had come into the prison with the butler.

When Yusuf had completed his prayer, he stood up and greeted the men, and then they sat together.

"Yusuf," the butler said. "I see you are a sincere man of kindness and wisdom. I have seen a strange dream and I want to ask you about it. It will not leave my mind.

I am in the palace kitchen courtyard. There are baskets and baskets of sweet white and red grapes. I am pressing them for wine."

"I also saw an odd dream," said the baker. "I can't stop thinking about it either. Please, help me too.

I am on the road. The sky is stormy and I am walking with a tray of bread on my head. The birds are flying around the bread and eating from it."

"I will help you," Yusuf said kindly. "That is part of the duty that my Lord has given me. Allah has given me the knowledge of many things, seen and unseen. You see, I have left the people who don't believe that Allah is One, and that we will meet Him on the world's Last Day. I have followed the way of my forefathers, of my father Yaqub and my grandfathers, Ishaq and Ibrahim. They have taught me that everything we see and know comes to us from the grace of Allah Who is creating us, and from nothing else, but most men do not know that and turn away from it, and are not grateful."

"But what about Isis, the Queen of the Earth, and Osiris, who taught us how to live?" asked the baker.

"You say "Isis" and "Osiris", but these are just names, with nothing behind them," Yusuf said. "My friends, just think about it for a while. What is

better? Many made-up gods that fight and destroy each other, or the all-powerful One God, Who knows and sees all things, because He is the Creator of all things?"

Yusuf's voice floated on deep silence, as the first rays of the sun shot over the prison wall. He put his hand on the butler's shoulder and gave him an affectionate squeeze.

"Now I will tell you about your dream. You will once again pour out wine for your master to drink, even though you now sit disgraced in prison."

"Thank you, thank you! May it be as you say, kind sir."

Yusuf turned then to the baker and put his hand on his shoulder. "And you, may Allah forgive you and give you patience, for you will hang from a cross for your crime, and the birds will eat from your head. The matter has been decided."

From the first words Yusuf spoke, the baker hung his head and wept, as though he already knew the meaning of his own dream.

Not many days passed before, indeed, the baker was dragged roughly out of the prison. He was never seen again. Then, a few more days after that, the butler was called back to the palace.

"Farewell, kind friend, Yusuf." the butler said. "I will always remember your generosity. Is there anything I can do for you?"

"Peace to you, my friend! When you see your king, remind him that I am here."

"Surely I can do that much for you, Yusuf. Goodbye."

He walked out of the prison into the sunshine, happy to be a free man. But, alas, once he had returned to the palace and to his former servant's duties, the thought of Yusuf never once crossed his mind, and Yusuf remained in prison.

But one evening years later, the butler overheard a conversation between the king and his close advisors.

"I saw a very strange dream," said the king.

"There were seven fine fat cows in a field. Seven weak, bony, starving cows were devouring the fat ones, skin, flesh and bone. Then there were seven full ripe green sheaves of wheat and then I saw seven dry, withered ones.

What on earth can such a dream mean? What do you think?"

The advisors shifted around uncomfortably, each one wishing he could interpret the king's dream, none wanting to appear ignorant.

"This is a most confusing dream, Your Excellency!"

The butler stood nearby with a goblet in his hand, listening. He suddenly remembered Yusuf, for the first time since he had left prison.

"It is I who can help you in this matter," he said. "I know of one highly skilled in the interpretation of dreams. Let me go in search of him, and I will come back and relate the interpretation to you."

Permission was granted and before long the butler was standing before Yusuf in prison.

"Yusuf, you always told us the truth! Our king has seen a dream. What does it mean, seven fat cows being devoured by seven starving ones? He saw seven full green sheaves of wheat, and seven dry withered ones. Tell us, what can this mean, so that I may return and let everyone know."

Without saying anything about his obviously forgotten and undelivered message, Yusuf said, "Your king's dream is a warning. Egypt will have seven years of rich harvests, and after that a seven-year drought will devour all the grain you've raised in the first seven years. You must utilise all your powers of farming for the next seven years, and protect all you grow like a treasure. Use as little as possible to meet your needs, and store the rest as it has grown, in the ears, to protect it from weevils. You must also store some away for planting. After the seven years of drought a year of deliverance will come when your harvests will again be bountiful. You will squeeze juices and press oils in abundance."

The butler returned to the king, who listened in wonder to the wise interpretation of his mysterious dream. "Bring him here to me at once. I must meet him and see him with my own eyes."

But when the butler once again stood before Yusuf in the prison, Yusuf said,

"No, I will not go with you. Go back and tell your master to find out first the truth from the ladies who cut their hands, so that he can see that I am without guilt."

The butler hurried back and related what he'd heard to the king. The king's eyebrows shot up. He called the women before him. "What happened when you asked Yusuf to do wrong?"

"We swear we saw nothing but absolute purity and modesty in his actions and his countenance," they said. "We were astonished."

Zulaykha stepped forward then. For all the years Yusuf had been in prison, not a single day had passed when she had not wept for him, when she had not gone near the prison hoping to see some sign of him, when she had not regretted her actions. She had grown thin and drawn from longing and lamentation, and her eyes had lost their lustre.

"Now may the truth be clear to everyone, after it has been concealed for years. It was I who sought to steal his goodness, his purity, his light, his very soul. A more true and virtuous man I have never known. And all the time he has been gone I have never spoken evil of him. I want him to know this. I have never betrayed him in his absence even though I betrayed him when he was in my presence. I am not free of blame - the soul sways towards evil, unless my Lord shows me mercy. May He forgive me and have mercy on me for what I have wrought."

She sat down and wept. The king and the other women looked on and for the first time they understood the depth of her pain.

In the prison, Yusuf was with the warden, who had grown to love him deeply in those years.

"Yusuf, the king's own messenger, came here to get you. Why did you not jump at the chance for freedom when it was handed to you?"

"I wanted my name to be cleared," answered Yusuf. "I wanted to leave prison on my own innocence, not because someone was pardoning me."

Back at the palace, the king had returned to his chambers. The women wrapped a shawl around Zulaykha and helped her back to her house.

The king summoned the butler again. "Bring Yusuf here to me at once! I want him for myself, to help me."

And this time, Yusuf left the prison with the butler and came at long last into the presence of the ruler of all of Egypt, the Hyksos king. The king stood up when they came in. He offered his hand and Yusuf took it warmly. With this simple gesture the king realised how trustworthy Yusuf was.

"Yusuf, you have more than proved your fidelity to us. We invite you to be among us with high honours, and we place all trust in you. Welcome!"

"Thank you, Your Excellency. I accept. But put me in charge of the harvests. Allah has given me knowledge to guard and preserve and protect. With His grace I can lead you safely through the trial that awaits you."

CHAPTER FOUR
Himself an Aziz

And so it was that Yusuf came from the land of Canaan to the land of Egypt, to be established as an honored and powerful figure, himself an Aziz and no longer the slave of one, with authority to do whatever he willed with the wealth of the kingdom.

Thus did Allah establish him in a position of power and possession in the land. And so it is that mercy is bestowed, as Allah wills, upon the doers of good, and their rewards are never lost. The boy who was drawn from the well and thrown into slavery became a chief minister in one of the greatest empires of that day and time. He could come and go as he pleased there, as if he were the master of it. Allah says, "Be!" and it is, it surely is.

Ah, but the world of the Next Life is even greater for those who believe and are constant and diligent in their actions.

Under Yusuf's firm hand, thousands upon thousands of sacks of grain from the fields of Egypt were harvested in the ear, just as they had grown. They were brought to the central granaries by boats all along the Nile River, and overland by camel, by donkey and by horse.

Every single sack was painstakingly counted and recorded by careful scribes with their reed brushes and boards. Then most were carted off to a separate room, where they were opened and poured into massive storage bins. The rest were hauled to another building, where the kernels were separated from the ear and then ground into flour to be baked into bread.

Yusuf never let it be forgotten that the prosperity would not last and finally, sure enough, came the drought. What was green became brown; what was lush became dry and brittle. Then, in the years of calamity that followed - just as he had said they would - his ministering proved a great source of comfort for all of Egypt and even for the surrounding countries, which purchased grain in great measure.

One day a band of men from Canaan appeared in the granary doorway. Yusuf heard their voices before he saw them, and he froze where he sat, for the voices were familiar, indeed, as familiar as his own. Every hair on the back of his neck stood out. His heart pounded. His mouth was dry. For years there had been an ache deep in his soul, an aching longing for his father and mother, and for his brother Binyamin. He often remembered the happy life he had left behind on that fateful day when he had set out with his brothers and had landed up in the bottom of the well. Now, at the mere sound of these familiar voices the ache rose up within him like a raging sea.

He turned in his chair and for a moment or two he watched them silently, reflecting on these men whom he now recognised for sure as his own half-brothers, whom he had not seen since the day he fell down into the well. They were so different, yet exactly the same as they had been. Though they were hard, fully grown men now, he could still glimpse their softer, boyish faces through the beards and the hardness, just as they had been.

The head scribe had greeted them, and was bringing them over to where Yusuf was sitting. By the time it had become necessary to speak to them, he had fully composed himself.

"Welcome," he smiled. "Where have you come from?"

He knew well there was no way they would recognise him. He had been a mere boy on that day they had last seen him. Now he was a grown man, with a full beard. They had long thought he must be dead or languishing away as a slave in some household or other. They never would have dreamed that he could have become a high official in another land.

Who can predict such things? Who could predict that a lowly acorn would become a great spreading oak tree, or that a tiny worm could become a brilliantly-coloured butterfly, or that a clot of blood could become a human being? Who could have predicted that many years later a helpless infant plucked by the Pharaoh's guards would grow up to liberate his people? Who could ever have predicted that hundreds of years after that, the unwanted orphan the Bedouin wet-nurses rejected could have grown up to be the final prophet of Allah? Yet Allah says, "Be!" and it is.

Rubin spoke for everyone. "We come from the land of Canaan."

Yusuf's mouth was dry. He trembled, remembering how Rubin had thrown Judah off of him as he lay terrified on the ground near the well. He had forgotten the blows and threats he had taken from his brothers on that day...but now every detail flooded back, and he felt a gloom of deep pain steal over his heart. And then the pain lifted as he remembered the inspiration he had heard that day so long before, alone in the bottom of the well:

"Yusuf, remember Us. We will not desert you.

You cannot understand now, but it will all become clear in the end. And you will one day tell your brothers about what they are doing to you, at a time when they do not know who you are." He found his voice. "Well, what brings you here to Egypt?"

He behaved as if he had never seen any of them. How could he trust men who had tossed their own brother into a well? Indeed, it was a feat of massive strength to keep himself hidden from the very ones who would have information about his dearly loved and longed-for father, and the half-brother he had not seen since he was barely a toddler. So he just uttered, "How are you faring in Canaan with this drought?"

"It is terrible. We are about to starve. We have nothing left but empty sacks, we have lost our livestock. We heard that you can sell us grain. Is it true?"

"Maybe. Who is it you have to feed?"

"We are ten brothers, the sons and grandsons of a prophet. Seven of us are married with children. We also have a half-brother, and our father is very old. Before the drought, we were prosperous, but now we have lost almost everything. Please help us."

"Why have you not brought your half-brother?"

"He is the youngest. We left him to care for our father."

Yusuf's heart skipped a beat, but his voice was steady. "Is your father ill?"

"No, but he is quite old and we didn't want to leave him alone."

"Very well," Yusuf said. "You may take provisions for yourselves and your families back home. I will give you provisions for your journey home, too, for I honor you as guests. If you bring your brother back, for I must see all the able-bodied men in your family, I'll give you an extra camel-load of grain."

"Sir, we thank you for your generosity."

"But," Yusuf went on, "you must know that if you do not bring your brother back, you'll get no more grain at all."

The brothers looked at each other, surprised.

"Sir, we will surely try and convince his father to let him come back with us."

Yusuf cringed when he heard the words, 'his father.' The father of this half-brother was their own father. What coldness, what cruelty was it that allowed them to speak that way?

They gave Yusuf the sack of copper and silver they had brought for the trade, and the bags of grain were loaded onto their camels. But when no one was looking, Yusuf had one of his servants put the sack of metals back in the pack from which they had been taken, and hide it under the sacks of grain so that they would not find it until they had returned home.

The brothers returned as quickly as they could to Canaan. They arrived just after dark, after their days and days of traveling, and they found Yaqub sitting beside a small fire near his tent. He had been relieved to hear the grunts and snarls of their laden camels approaching. Rubin ran to him and knelt beside him, with Judah following close behind.

"*Abana*, we've brought grain for all our families. But we will get no more at all unless we return with Binyamin. He says he must himself see every man in our family."

"*Abana*," Judah said. "Send him with us, or we will get no more help. We will guard him perfectly."

Yaqub stared coldly at his sons when he heard those words. "Shall I trust him with you after I trusted his brother with you?"

Judah cried out as if he'd been struck. He leapt to his feet and stormed off, away from the circle of light thrown by the fire.

"*Abana*," Rubin persisted. "We'll take very good care of him, really."

Yaqub turned away. "Allah is the best of protectors," he said, "and He is the Most Merciful of the Merciful. I hope Allah will show me mercy by protecting my youngest son and not allowing another catastrophe to befall our family. May Allah be his protector."

Just then Simeon rushed over to them. "Look at this! I was unpacking the saddlebags and found the sack of metals. Judah, didn't you give it to the official in Egypt as a guarantee?"

"You saw me give it to him," Judah replied, returning from the dark shadows around the firelight. "He must have put it back, to assure us that if we bring Binyamin, he will sell us more grain and even give us extra. *Abana*, don't you see? You must give your permission."

"I'll never send him unless you swear a solemn oath in the name of Allah that you will certainly bring him back to me, unless you yourselves are surrounded and made powerless. And Allah is witness to all I say. I have assigned the whole matter to Allah, and anyone who wants the Best of Trustees will do the same."

The stone water-jars were still in their places, and remembered in this moment the words that had slipped out of Yaqub's mouth many years ago, when these same sons wanted to take Yusuf on an outing with them. "…there are wolves…" he had said. The boys had come back without Yusuf, carrying his blood-stained tunic and crying fake tears, uttering a dark lie about the wolves. "Calamity depends on the words that come from the mouth," the water-jugs had whispered, and now they whispered it again.

The brothers swore their solemn oath in the name of Allah.

After a few days, as the brothers prepared for their return to Egypt with Binyamin, Yaqub called them to him in his tent.

"My sons, listen to me. When you get to the city, you must not all enter through the same gate. You are a big group and you must not draw attention to yourselves. People might envy you because you are ten strong brothers. Enter in smaller groups through different gates. That will be better."

He turned away, and sat down. His voice faltered. "O, but of what use are my feeble words against the Will of Allah? All we can do is trust in Him, for He is the arranger of all affairs. Yet we must do our best."

The brothers left, and he went back to his prayers.

When finally the brothers arrived in Egypt, they did as Yaqub had asked: they entered the city through different gates in smaller groups. But in fact that did not benefit them at all in the planning of Allah. It was but a necessity

Yaqub had insisted on for them. Though he knew well the Power and Supremacy of the Plans of Allah, still he understood our responsibility for taking whatever means are at our disposal as we prepare ourselves to receive His manifestations upon us.

It was his great ancestress Hajar who had demonstrated this so beautifully as she ran between Safa and Marwa in her need for water. That running of hers had nothing really to do with the eventual manifestation of the miraculous waters that even then were gushing around in the depths beneath her feet, and yet, her running was a demonstration of her complete and utter faith in Allah.

The eleven met up near the granaries and came into Yusuf's presence together.

"Welcome, welcome," Yusuf said.

"Thank you, kind sir," they replied. "We have brought our brother, as you requested."

Yusuf smiled and said, "Good. I am pleased. Now let him come close to me. I want to meet him."

Rubin pushed Binyamin to the front.

Binyamin! The first glimpse of his little brother since that fateful day all those years ago must have shaken Yusuf to the core, yet not a trace of that showed or could even be heard in his voice.

He wanted to shout, "O, how handsome you have grown!" But instead, his steady voice said, "So, this is the half-brother, the one who stays at home looking after his ageing father."

He wanted to throw his arms around him and weep for joy, but instead he kept his distance and held his head high in the manner of the high official of Egypt that he was.

If you had been close to him you might have seen the veins in his neck standing out, or the minuscule muscles of his jaw working, or even a bead or two of sweat on his brow.

You'd have felt the blood pounding in his ears and in his breast. You'd have noticed that he was breathing very carefully, as if he might break into a thousand pieces.

But all he said was, "Come, let's eat together."

They entered the banquet hall in the king's quarters. The brothers all found places together around an enormous table, leaving Binyamin alone at the far end with an empty chair beside him. Yusuf sat there, happy, even trembling, to be close to him yet still suffering under the weight of his secret.

"My friend," Yusuf asked. "Why do you look so sad?"

"If my brother Yusuf were alive, he would be sitting here beside me."

After the meal, Yusuf sent the brothers to their sleeping quarters. Binyamin was left behind, and Yusuf took him to a corner of the garden, under a lush grapevine. They settled themselves onto a grass mat.

"Tell me about yourself. Tell me about this father you stay home to care for."

Binyamin began slowly at first, shyly, to tell Yusuf about himself, but soon the quality of Yusuf's listening drew him out, and before long he had spilled out his whole story, how his favourite brother had disappeared, how it seemed the brothers had claimed he'd been taken by a wolf and he had never returned, how the once happy days of his childhood had come to a close on that morning when he awoke to find his father weeping into his brother's favourite tunic, bloodstained.

Yusuf listened patiently, as if every single word was the first and only word his brother would ever utter. But it became harder and harder to listen and keep still.

Finally, he asked, "Would you take me in place of your brother who died?"

Binyamin's jaw dropped. "What?! Take you in his place?" All the colour was gone from his face. "No one," he stammered, and his voice broke. "No one could ever take the place of my brother Yusuf, no matter how grand a person he may be."

Yusuf flew to his feet. "But Binyamin, I am your brother Yusuf! I was thrown into a well, not devoured by wolves."

Binyamin stared at him, unable to move. Yusuf leaned toward him, assuring him, "I am your brother. It's me, Yusuf!"

Binyamin flung himself to his feet and held his brother away at arm's length and looked deeply into his face. Suddenly the years fell away and for an instant he was a little child again, looking at the face of his big brother under the olive tree in Canaan. Long-held anguish leapt from his belly and breast and he threw his arms around Yusuf, nearly knocking him over.

"Shhh, they must not hear us." They locked their arms around each other briefly and then sat down again to avoid calling attention to themselves in any way.

"Listen, Binyamin.' Yusuf whispered. "Forget about what our brothers have done, for now. Don't let them know our secret. And don't be concerned about any unexpected things that may happen here. Go now, join our brothers in the sleeping quarters. We'll see each other in the morning. Be careful! Don't give away our secret, not yet."

Yusuf went off to pray. He was deeply happy about his reunion with his brother, and yet profoundly shaken by the chasm of grief he had encountered in him. He worried about his father. Then, some say, he felt the presence of the Angel Jibril. "O Jibril! Is there any news of my father Yaqub?"

And Jibril answered him. "Yes. Allah gave him the patience to endure this calamity bravely and He has subjected him to grieving for you. But he is remembering Allah in his grief, and not complaining."

"And how deep is his sorrow?"

"It is deeper than the bottom of the sea, deeper than the darkness of the night sky, deeper than the sadness of a father who loses seventy sons, one by one."

"And what is the reward for it?"

"It is the highest reward of Allah's Presence in Paradise, because he never once lost his faith in Him."

O Allah, You who are the Planner of all affairs, my Source and my Sustainer, increase my gratitude! You have reunited me at long last with my brother, and I give thanks. And I beg of You, please let me be reunited with my dear father, Yaqub. I cannot bear to see Binyamin go away from me. If he could stay here, a way may open for my father to come as well. Please, O Opener of Ways, inspire me, show me how to keep Binyamin here at my side without letting his brothers know who I am.

They say Yusuf felt the angel depart, and he lay down to sleep. We can imagine him waking up later, getting up, washing his face and his hands and his feet, and kneeling again to pray.

When Yusuf opened his eyes, they fell upon the king's golden goblet, which was being carried on a tray by a passing servant. Before he knew what he was doing, Yusuf had leapt from his straw mat and had snatched the goblet from the tray.

Hiding the goblet deep in his robes, he went to meet his brothers, who were waiting to have their camels loaded with grain and set off for Canaan.

"Well, I hope you slept well last night." He gave them a jovial smile.

"Indeed we did, kind sir. Thank you very much! We are grateful for your hospitality."

While they were talking, the servants were loading up the camels with sacks of grain. Yusuf turned away from them to attend to another matter and when he turned back, he saw they had walked over to inspect the load of another camel. He slipped the goblet into one of Binyamin's saddlebags before anyone had a chance to see him.

The camels were loaded, the good-byes and thanks were said, and the eleven were on their way. But before they had reached the gates of the city, a group of sentries came racing up behind them.

"Stop! You are thieves!"

They stopped, dumbfounded. "What?"

Walking up to the sentries, Rubin said, "What has been stolen?"

"The King's golden goblet is missing. Whoever finds it will have a bull-camel's load of grain, guaranteed."

"By Allah, you know us. We have not come into your country to cause mischief, and we are certainly not thieves!"

"Well, if you turn out to be lying, what do you say the penalty should be?"

"The penalty? Why, according to us, the one found to be guilty would have to remain with you as a slave. That is how we would punish a thief."

"Very well then, so be it. We had better conduct a thorough search, but let's not do it here on the road. Come back to the store-houses. The Aziz himself will do it."

When they came in Yusuf was careful not to look into Binyamin's eyes, but prayed secretly that he would remember the warning he had given him the night before.

He began the search with

the bags of the eldest, Rubin, while the brothers looked on. When he found nothing unusual in Rubin's bags, he moved on to the other brothers' bags, one by one. Finally he came to Binyamin's bag, and made as though he was willing to abandon the search, but the brothers insisted he continue.

They searched the first pouch and found nothing. Yusuf opened up the second one, reached inside, and pulled out the goblet. The brothers gasped. For a long time, nobody said anything.

"Whose bag is this?" Yusuf asked.

"It is mine, sir." Binyamin stared at the ground, looking for all the world like a thief being caught red-handed.

Rubin's face darkened with scorn. "Binyamin had it all along!"

"Well, that's no surprise, Rubin." Judah flung his satchel to the floor. "His brother was a thief before him, remember?"

Would your heart not pound and your cheeks not flare up hot if you heard such words – if your brothers had abused and wronged you and now tried to raise themselves up by accusing you? But Yusuf kept the affair locked inside his heart. His voice was firm.

"Binyamin," he said, "I charge you with theft! According to the punish—ment you yourselves have suggested, I forbid you to leave Egypt. You will stay here, and become a royal slave. Guard! Bring the chains."

"O great Aziz," Rubin said. "Please, I beg you to take one of us in his place. His father is so old, and will grieve bitterly if he does not come back to him. We see that you are one who excels in good - please help us!"

Yusuf scowled. "Allah forbid! To take another in his place would be wrong. No, he must himself pay for his crime, you yourselves have asserted."

For the first time, I looked straight in Binyamin's eyes and understood that his brother was complete agreement with the course of affairs; tone and behavior protected their secret entirely.

When they saw no hope changing Yusuf's mind,

went off to talk. The guard arrived with the chains and took Binyamin, who hung his head in a kind of sweet submission that looked to the brothers, for whom it was intended, like a guilty shame.

"Look," Rubin said. "You know that *Abana* has bound us by an oath in the name of Allah to bring Binyamin back...and now we have failed him again...just like we failed him before when we didn't bring Yusuf back. May Allah help us!"

His voice broke then, and he struggled to continue. "As I am the oldest, I will stay here too. I will not go home until Father permits me to or until Allah commands me, and He is the best to command. You go back without me. Tell him that Binyamin stole the cup, and that we were surrounded and could do nothing to change the official decision of this land. Tell him that we weren't aware of the unseen when we made the promise we made to him. Tell him to come here himself and ask in this city, and those among the caravan we travelled with, and he will find that you are telling the truth. We can only bear witness to what we know."

"But Rubin," Judah asked. "What about you? What will you do?"

"Just go without me. Don't worry about me. I'll find something. Just tell my wife not to worry."

CHAPTER FIVE
"YOU Are Yusuf?"

Reluctantly, the brothers parted with Rubin and made the journey back to Canaan. When they arrived, their parents and wives and children gathered around them while they dismounted, offering skins of water and greetings. Suddenly Yaqub went pale. "Where is Binyamin?"

"Binyamin is being held as a thief in the land of Egypt."

Yaqub fell to his knees, all the colour drained from his face. Everyone started talking at once.

"Binyamin? A thief? Impossible!"

"Whatever are you talking about?"

"Why did Rubin stay behind?"

Judah pushed closer to his father. "Just wait a minute and let us tell you. As we were leaving, a crier came up behind us and accused us of stealing the king's golden cup. They took us back to the storehouses and our bags were all searched by the official who had sold us the grain. They suspected us because we had been to a banquet in the king's quarters the night before, and the goblet was found missing the next morning. The official searched every one of our bags and could find nothing at all until he came to the last bag - Binyamin's bag," he smirked, "and there it was. We all stood there with our mouths gaping, and Binyamin just stood there staring at the floor."

Levi continued, "Before the official had started the search, one of the guards asked us what we thought the punishment should be for the one in whose possession the goblet was found. Rubin said that according to our customs, the owner of the stolen item would hold the thief as a slave."

Simeon stepped up. "When the goblet was found in Binyamin's bag the official charged him with theft. We begged him to keep one of us in his place but he refused to even consider it."

"But why did Rubin stay behind?" his wife asked. "When is he coming back?"

"We swore a solemn oath before Allah that we would bring Binyamin back unless we ourselves were surrounded and helpless," Judah said. "Well, that's just what happened. We were surrounded, and we were powerless. We tried to get them to release him, but they would not. We weren't aware of the unseen when we made the promise we made to you. We can only bear witness to what we know. Rubin says he will stay in Egypt until *Abana* gives him permission to return or until Allah commands him to come back."

Yaqub sat like a rock, his face tight. His wife Rachel stood behind him, holding his shoulder.

"Years ago," he said, "you asked me to believe a wolf had eaten my son Yusuf. And now you ask me to believe that Binyamin has stolen something from the king of Egypt."

Judah's face was red, the red that comes from a long-simmering guilty conscience.

"You can go and learn for yourself from the people of the caravan and the city that we are telling the truth."

"Judah," Yaqub said darkly. "You have made something horrible seem good to you. For me, there is nothing left but to beg Allah for patience and more patience, and still more patience. All I can do is trust in His goodness, in His wisdom, and trust that someday He will bring all three of my sons back to me. Indeed my Lord is All-Knowing, All-Wise!"

He turned away from them utterly, and left the tent, Rachel at his side. As he passed through the flap to the outside, his family heard him sob, "O, how I ache for Yusuf."

Judah leapt for the flap. "For the sake of Allah! Will you never stop weeping over Yusuf until you die?!"

Yaqub, peace and blessings be

upon him, stopped, stunned. "Judah, I complain of my grief only to Allah, and I know from Allah's kindness that which you do not know. Perhaps you could be more respectful to your father."

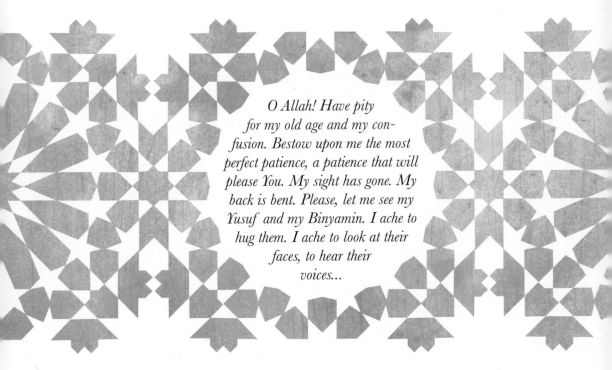

O Allah! Have pity for my old age and my con- fusion. Bestow upon me the most perfect patience, a patience that will please You. My sight has gone. My back is bent. Please, let me see my Yusuf and my Binyamin. I ache to hug them. I ache to look at their faces, to hear their voices...

Rachel led him out into the garden, and from that day on, his eyes grew white with weeping.

The next morning Simeon and Judah found their father still on his knees in the garden.

"Good morning, *Abana*. Are you feeling better today?"

"Allah be praised. ......My sons, I want you to return to Egypt."

"Return to Egypt?"

"Yes. Go back and scour the city for Yusuf. I have a feeling he is still alive. We must never give up on the soothing Mercy of Allah. No one gives up on it except those who have no faith."

Before the sun was high in the sky the brothers were once again on the road to Egypt.

"Do you think the official will receive us?" Levi asked his older brother.

"Only Allah knows. All we can do is try," answered Judah.

Simeon said, "Our father is crazed with grief. What else can we do?"

"Well, in any case I think we can do nothing until we find Rubin."

Actually, Rubin found them as they were wandering the souqs looking for him. They told him what happened when they had arrived home without

إِنَّمَا أَشْكُو بَثِّي وَحُزْنِي إِلَى اللَّهِ وَأَعْلَمُ مِنَ اللَّهِ مَا لَا تَعْلَمُونَ

Binyamin.

"You should see him, Rubin. His eyes are white with weeping. He spent the whole night on his knees in the garden. He insisted we come back here to find Yusuf!"

"He says he 'feels it in his bones' that somebody here may know something about where he is," said Levi.

"What else do we have except to try and do as he says?" said Simeon.

They spent the rest of the daylight hours prowling around the ancient crowded streets of the city, in and out of shops, down into cellars and out onto balconies and up onto roofs. They asked everyone they saw, man, woman, child, but found not a scrap of a clue.

The next morning, soon after dawn, they went to the storehouses. They found Yusuf sitting on a bench near the massive wooden doors. He stood up graciously when they drew near.

"So, you have returned. What brings you back?"

Rubin spoke. "O Aziz! Our family is in great distress, our wives, our children... We have lost all our resources. Two of us are detained in Egypt, and a third is long lost. And our father is broken with grief, yet his faith in the mercy of Allah is unshaken. He has sent us."

"We have but worthless goods to offer in exchange, but please, sell us more grain," said Judah.

"Think of it as charity," said Simeon. "You know Allah rewards the charitable."

Yusuf said nothing, and the brothers, all ten of them, shifted uncomfortably. He sat down again.

"Please, Sir, we beg of you to help us," said Rubin.

Yusuf allowed the woven cloth to slip from his head. "Are you aware of what you have done to your brothers Yusuf and Binyamin in your ignorance?"

There was a moment of stunned silence.

Yusuf?

How does he know about Yusuf?

Has Binyamin told him something?

The old images of that fateful day flooded back into their memories with a clarity and immediacy they'd never felt before. They stared at him, and he cast his own steady gaze into their eyes, one face at a time, as the recognition dawned on them. *Yusuf? It couldn't be. But yet…how? How could he possibly have become a high official in Egypt?*

Rubin stepped forward. "You are Yusuf? How did you get here? How did you get out of the well?"

"I am Yusuf, and this is my brother, Binyamin." At that moment Binyamin emerged from the shadows of the storehouse. Yusuf pushed the brothers away from him, extended his hand to his full-brother, and drew him before the others. He looked each brother in the face and said,

"Allah has been gracious to us. You see that when a person is conscious of Him and patient in adversity, He does not fail to reward him. All praise to the Lord of the Worlds."

The brothers stared, incredulous, dangling between doubt and certainty. Vivid memories of the abuse they had heaped upon their brother flooded into them, with waves of fear about what the consequences of their actions would be. Could this really be Yusuf standing before them?

Can you imagine, around two thousand years later, how the Meccans cowered in their houses as Muhammad, may Allah bless him and give him peace, rode into their city, the city in which they had heaped abuse and murder on him and his family and followers? What would he do to them now that he was victorious over them?

Simeon's eyes were wet and his voice shook. "By Allah, Yusuf, surely has He preferred you over us, and we have clearly been in the wrong all these years!"

Remember all those years before, when they grumbled and accused their father of thinking Yusuf and his brother were better than they were?

Yusuf reassured him. "There is no blame on you this day, Simeon, nor upon any of you. May Allah forgive you, and He is the Best of Forgivers, and the Most Merciful of the Merciful."

The brothers' hearts opened, then, as did even the hearts of the cowering Quraysh in their houses a few thousand years later, on that day in Mecca. Muhammad's assurance, may Allah bless him and give him peace, was, "I say to you as Yusuf said to his brothers, 'No blame on you this day. Allah will forgive you, as He is the Most Merciful of the Merciful.'"

Then Judah, the same Judah who had grabbed Yusuf so long before and thrown him on the ground, and then in his heart of hearts had never passed a day without regretting it, though his bravado would never have let him say as much, and though he had accused Yusuf of being a thief to unload all his own guilt onto him, Judah was the one who jumped up first and grabbed him again, this time for a different reason.

"Yusuf. Yusuf! I see that same look in your eye that I saw when you were just a boy." He buried his face in the crook of Yusuf's neck and wept. "Forgive me, dear brother, forgive me for hurting you. I have never been able to forget it, how I threw you on the ground that day. I am sorry for calling you a thief. Forgive me, please forgive me."

The brothers crowded around him and Binyamin, most of them weeping now and jostling with one another for the chance to hug them and kiss them both. Levi stayed behind, his face hard and unmoving. But when Yusuf sought him out and embraced him, he dissolved into tears.

"By Allah, Yusuf," Judah said. "You have been elevated far above us, and we have done terrible things against you. Please forgive us."

"Yes, Yusuf, please!" said Rubin.

Yusuf's polished heart had burned away their betrayal. Even Judah's most recent accusation of his being a thief, which had slashed him and re-opened long-healed pain, could have no lasting substance in the clear illuminated chambers of his heart.

"Of all those who show mercy, Judah, the Most Merciful is Allah, and He will forgive you. As for me, I am happy to hear your apologies, and I am grateful to be reunited with you. But I am very worried about *Abana*."

He quickly wriggled out of his shirt, which was woven of the finest Egyptian cotton and dyed with subtle hues of blue, green, orange, and yellow.

"Go at once to Canaan, Rubin. Cast my shirt over his eyes and he will come. He will come to me seeing. Then return, all of you. Bring your wives..." His voice broke and for a moment he couldn't continue. "....your children, my mother Rachel."

As he accepted Yusuf's shirt, did Rubin recall how, all those years before, they had stripped Yusuf of a different shirt before tossing him into the well?

Leaving Binyamin with Yusuf a second time, and carrying his shirt, the ten brothers left the clamour of the city and set off for Canaan.

That very day, Yaqub was praying alone in his tent. The sun had risen and its rays were filtering in upon him through the open flaps. He had been up for hours, weeping and praying. His robe was soaked and stained with tears. All of a sudden, he stood up, changed his clothes, and walked out into the clear morning air.

Rubin's, Simeon's, and Judah's wives were there in the yard near the fountain doing laundry.

"Look. He's coming out of his tent."

"Poor thing. It's the first time in a few days that he's been in the sunlight."

Judah's wife wrung out the last shirt and hung it on a line to dry. "What will become of him, I wonder? He will die of grieving."

Binyamin's wife ran up to him. "Good morning, *Abana*. How are you today? Can I get you anything?"

"Yusuf is near! I feel his presence, my daughter."

She took his arm and led him to the fountain so he might wash his face.

"*Abana*, what did you just say?"

"Yusuf's scent is reaching me. He is near me, I know it! ….Probably if you didn't think me feeble-minded, you'd believe me."

"*Abana*, by Allah, you are still in your same old delusion. Yusuf has been gone for years."

Rachel came out of her tent just then. She had heard the entire conversation.

"Come on, there is bread." She and Binyamin's wife took him inside. The others just shook their heads and went back to their laundry.

It was almost fifteen days after this when, soon after dawn, Yaqub ran out to the dunes. Sure enough, there was a caravan approaching. He sensed that one rider was outstripping all the others, leaving a trail of flying sand behind him. With his heart leaping, Yaqub waited, and soon the rider came close enough for the voice to reach him.

"*Abati! Abati!*" It was Rubin. "We found him, *Abati*! We found him! He sent you his shirt!"

Was this the same Rubin, all those years before, who had held out that other, goat-blood-stained shirt as pitiful evidence for a monstrous lie? Well, no, it was not the same Rubin. For Allah's forgiveness changes all things.

Rubin jumped down off his camel and ran toward Yaqub. He threw Yusuf's tunic over his face. "*Abati*. Yusuf said to throw it over your eyes and you will come to him seeing."

Yaqub buried his face in the shirt, weeping. "Mighty and Majestic Allah!" he gasped. "How deep is Your Mercy and Your Generosity!" His whole body shook as the scent of his long-lost son swept through every fibre of his being. Not just an inkling of scent, as he had experienced from the moment his sons had set out for home carrying the shirt, but the full overwhelming scent. Years of longing and anguish simply vanished away, and an almost unbearable joy filled him.

Rubin looked on, catching his breath. Finally Yaqub looked up at him. "Did I not tell you, Rubin? Did I not tell you that I know things about His Mercy that you do not know?!"

"*Abati*, we did a grievous wrong to you and Yusuf. Please forgive us, and pray that Allah will forgive us."

"Rubin, I can see again, it's just as he said."

By this time the others had caught up and jumped off their camels. They surrounded their father, all of them talking at once. He stared at them, one by one, marvelling at their faces, which he hadn't been able to see for so long.

"*Abana*, Yusuf is the official who sold us the grain." said Judah. "He never let us know who he was. That's why he insisted on Binyamin coming, and Binyamin never stole the goblet."

"*Abana*, please forgive us and ask for forgiveness for us."

"We were so wrong, *Abana*."

"Indeed I will ask, and keep asking, for He is the best of Forgivers, Most Merciful. Your words are splendid music to my ears, almost as sweet as the news of Yusuf!"

News of the brothers' arrival spread fast to their families. Binyamin's son came running. "Where is my *aba*?"

Rubin reached down and swept the boy up into his powerful arms. "Don't you worry a bit. You are going to see your aba soon enough. Look!" He reached into a pocket and drew something out. "He sent you a sweet from Egypt."

The boy struggled free and ran with the sweet to his mother, who was standing beside Rachel.

The rest of the day rang with laughter and merriment as they started packing up their belongings for the move to Egypt. After a day, or it may have been two, they set off - Yaqub and Rachel, Binyamin's wife and children, and the brothers with their wives and children. With the elderly mothers and fathers of some of the wives, they were almost a hundred strong. And you can well imagine the joy they might have felt as they travelled.

But the laughter and the excitement they had lived in Canaan was nothing compared to what they were to live when they were to be finally reunited with Yusuf in the glorious land of Egypt!

45

CHAPTER SIX
A Magnificent Reunion

"Your family?"

Yusuf had gone to the king to ask permission for his family to settle in Egypt.

"I've never once thought about you having a family. You came to us alone, from outside, and then became one of us...I'm not sure I want to give you up to another family." He gave Yusuf a playful slap on the back and walked over to the window. He turned, smiling, and his arms swung in a wide sweep in front of him.

"But of course I give my permission. And I will give more than that - I will give houses and animals and carpets and cooking pots too. And when they arrive, a grand feast for everyone! You are deeply loved in the land of Egypt, Yusuf. I am certain we will all love your family as well."

So the preparations began for the great arrival. Blazing ovens were bursting with roasting meat. In Yusuf's own banquet hall and the surrounding gardens, long low tables adorned with huge baskets of flowers appeared with richly upholstered cushions on either side. Cooks turned out tray after tray of glistening sweets in the palace kitchen. Servants rushed in with piles of fresh linens and servants rushed out with trays of silver bowls and emerald-studded goblets.

Even the streets of the city were ablaze with excited preparations, as everyone had been invited to the feast. The homes that the king had promised for the family were being furnished with carpets and feather beds, oil lamps and brooms and pots. Sheep and goats and chickens were gathered and herded and settled into their new quarters, and soon everything was ready.

A crier had been sent out into the desert to watch for the approaching caravan and announce its arrival. It was in the late afternoon when the cry sounded and warm sea-waves of excitement surged through the streets, the lanes, the by-ways, and the alleys.

Within minutes watchers and welcomers

with hearts full of expectation surged onto roofs and balconies.

"Think of it! Ah, dear Yusuf...how many years has it been since he has seen his old father?"

"Grandma! If I were Yusuf, I would pick up my father and hug him and hug him like this." He ran to her and threw his arms around her, nearly knocking her over.

From the palace a troop of colourful jugglers, acrobats, and singers was making its way toward the gates of the city to greet the newcomers. Children were running along after them, laughing like gulls.

Behind them came Yusuf with Binyamin on one side, and the Hyksos king on the other. When they reached the gates of the city they waited with the other nobles of the land on a platform which had been erected especially for this occasion.

At last the caravan came into full view. At the head of it was old Yaqub, peace be upon him, sitting astride the lead camel. Yusuf felt a thrill of joy when he saw how straight and tall his father sat in that camel saddle.

It seemed to take forever for the caravan to draw near. They each sat staring across the distance as the minutes passed, and still they seemed so far away from each other. Finally Yusuf couldn't contain himself any longer. He jumped off the platform and began running toward the caravan.

Yaqub ordered his camel to sit and when it did he hit the ground just as Yusuf reached him. He grabbed his son and swung him around as if he were still the boy he had been when they were separated. Both men were sobbing and neither one spoke. Even if words could have been said there weren't any big enough and there was no need for them anyway.

Everyone watched, some weeping, some spellbound, with their mouths open, some laughing for joy. It seemed as if the world itself had stopped turning for this moment, and the air was electric with the presence of the angels who had come at Jibril's bidding, to witness.

The sun was about to set. The full moon was rising fat and orange on the opposite horizon. The hungry desert honey badgers dropped their daily sundown search for food and fell silent suddenly, to listen. The whole universe witnessed as what had been sundered was now joined, and what had been severed was now healed.

Now hugging, now kissing each other's faces, now holding each other at arm's length to look, the two men made their way back to the gates of the city.

"O King of Egypt, please welcome my father Yaqub, the

prophet of Allah." And, in the long-ago way which was their way of showing respect, the King of Egypt bowed down to Yaqub, led him to a carpet and pillows at the centre of the platform, and seated him there. A lovely glistening bronze-skinned servant girl came and poured out water from a silver pitcher into a brass bowl for him to wash his hands and face after his long journey. A boy waved long graceful palm fronds for a cooling breeze.

Rachel's camel had arrived by now, and Yusuf ran to help her down. Their embrace was long, and still, and tender. He led her to the platform and seated her beside his father.

The brothers greeted Binyamin like they had never greeted him before. When Binyamin's son saw this he broke free from his mother and ran to join them. Years of rough treatment and rejection had ended, and the child was like a bird set free from a cage. Binyamin reached his wife and the other children, who crawled all over him in delight.

The singers, with their drums and their tambourines, began to sing about other joyful reunions of olden days. The acrobats were leaping, the jugglers cavorting and prancing, and there was not a single heart there that was not vaulting for joy in its breast.

Maybe an hour passed, maybe two, but at last it was time to continue on to Yusuf's mansion, where the banquet was waiting for them. Forty ebony-skinned men, handsome, straight-backed, stately and strong, came, surrounded the platform, lifted it up gracefully to their shoulders, and floated it toward the palace. The throngs of people parted to let it and the caravan pass, blowing kisses, tossing flowers, calling out prayers and good wishes and shimmering glances of light.

Just at the foot of the palace hill, they met a procession of animals. The forty-men-acting-as-one-man put down the platform gently. Yaqub and his family watched in delight as a pair of glossy jet-black leopards pranced at the front, followed by a lofty and lissome giraffe, a delightfully arrogant ostrich, a light-footed gazelle, and finally, a pair of stalwart pure-white oxen with a carved olive-wood yoke. The desert-dwellers were transfixed. Binyamin's son

wanted to jump down from the platform but Yusuf caught him just in the nick of time and held him back.

"Not so fast, my boy! Let's go on to the palace and see what's for dinner. You must be hungry."

The platform rose again into the air and continued its lofty flight through the streets. The people were overjoyed...it was easy to see the love they all felt for Yusuf.

Soon they were set down again, at the entrance to the palace gardens. The honored guests made their way along narrow paths that passed beneath branches heavy with dates and pomegranates to the wide door of the banquet hall.

A servant led the wives and families of Yusuf's brothers into the hall, while Yusuf himself led his parents and brothers to see his private quarters and the quarters that had been prepared for them.

"I give thanks to Allah for this most joyful of reunions!" declared Yusuf to his family. "I have spent years in longing, but I never once gave up hope that Allah would reunite us at last."

Yusuf faced his father and placed his hands on his shoulders, looking him eagerly in the eyes. "*Abana*, enter Egypt in utmost safety, and find here your home. I welcome you and all the members of our family to this land, where you will be, if it pleases Allah, guarded well and made to be comfortable, and may you live here long and fully in His grace."

Yaqub embraced his son. "All praise to Allah, the Lord of the Worlds, the Best of Planners. I, too, wept and prayed for years, my son. Nor did I once give up hope. And now I bow down to you in honour and respect,

50

O Vizier of Egypt!"

Bowing down before another was their way of showing respect and honour at that time. That was long, long ago, before the Message of Allah was completed with the Last Prophet, Muhammad, peace and blessings be upon him. Now we have learned that we must bow down only to Allah, the Lord of All Worlds.

But this is their story, from their time. When the brothers heard their father's words, they rushed up to bow to him, and then his mother bowed to him.

"My Father," Yusuf said. "This is the dream of long ago, when the sun and the moon and the stars bowed down before me...it seems like yesterday. Allah has certainly been generous with me: He took me out of the dark prison and made it clear to all that I was not guilty...He made me a man of standing and responsibility in this land...and now He has by His subtle planning brought all of you out of the desert to live here with me...all this after Shaytan had caused enmity between my brothers and me. Allah truly knows every big and small thing. He knows best what is good for people, and arranges every affair. We cannot fathom His plans but truly He is Mighty and Majestic."

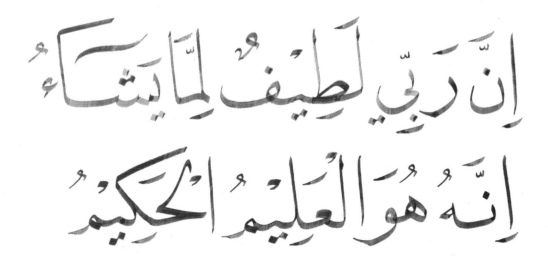

"All praise to Allah, Mighty and Majestic Allah!" declared Yaqub.

Yusuf led his family back to the banquet hall and seated his parents in the highest honour. The brothers sat on bright cushions before huge round tables covered with roasted chickens, pots of lamb and rice, trays of figs stuffed with walnuts, loaves of crusty bread, and piles of syrupy sweets, arranged around the throne in a wide semi-circle. The huge hall was filled with tables, and so was the garden, as everyone in the city had been invited to the welcoming banquet, and they all came, too, dressed in their finest and expecting the best.

While everyone was eating, the musicians sang the tale of another feast of long ago, a feast that celebrated the return of an ancient ruler from exile. A hush fell over the room and when the song had ended, the silence grew even

O Allah! You have made me an aziz here in Egypt, and You have taught me a tremendous share of the interpretation of dreams and events. O Creator of the heavens and the earth, You are my Protector, and my Sustainer, in this world and in the next. When I die, take my soul on the religion of the prophets in a state of submission to You, and unite me with the righteous.

deeper.

Yusuf stood in this silence and opened his hands and raised his eyes upwards.

The angels, who had been present from the beginning, were pleased by the family's reunion, subhanAllah.

Shaytan, who had tried his best to make Yaqub and Yusuf, peace and blessings be upon them both, forget the grace and largesse of Allah, went off in defeat and utter dejection, alhamdulillah.

We, having heard their story, may we, by the grace of Allah Mighty and Majestic, comprehend it and learn our lessons from it, inshaAllah, for it is truly a fountain of lessons for people of every age.

And Zulaykha? No one knows for sure. Some say her longing for him led her to true knowledge of Allah. Some even say that when he met her that day he came out of prison, he touched her and her beauty and youth returned, and they married.

Muhammad, may Allah bless him and give him peace, was given this story as a comfort and a sign. From it, he could learn that just as the blessed prophet Yusuf's state of betrayal and tribulation, peace upon him, would transform into a state of victory and success, so too would his tribulation transform, may Allah bless him and give him peace. Alhamdulillah we are still living in the radiance of that triumph! May Allah increase our understanding and our gratitude!

May the blessings and the peace of Allah be upon all who read this telling. May it awaken a thirst for the real narrative in the Glorious Qur'an, which is but a doorway into infinite realms of unending meaning, alhamdulillah.

If anything I have written be a mistake, the fault is mine and I ask Allah Mighty and Majestic for forgiveness. If anything I have written is a seed of deeper knowledge, it is entirely from Allah, Who wants us to know Him.

AFTERWORD

The Majestic Qur'an is at the very heart of this project, and Allah Mighty and Majestic opened it for us first, some twenty years ago, through the painstaking and precise work of a beloved and renowned scholar of tafseer and Arabic rhetoric, Sheikh Ali Hani. And that was made accessible for us through the patient and sensitive translations of Sheikh Sohail Hanif, sentence-by-sentence, through long hours with the text and further research from Sheikh Ali's stack of Arabic tomes by leading tafsir scholars.

Then, after many years of its becoming a beloved audio production, the project to produce it as a book was born. My most fervent duas for the perfect illustrator were answered in the work of MforMoon, and, as if that were not enough, Allah led us to calligrapher Na'eel Cajee. Mashallah, he completed a beautiful circle by revealing that he too had studied Surah Yusuf with Sheikh Sohail and Arabic and tafsir with Sheikh Ali, back in the day, in Amman Jordan. Allah says BE! And it is, it surely is!

Allahu Akbar, alhamdulillah.

Shaykh Ali Hani, a descendant of the Companion Jabir bin Abdullah, may God be pleased with him, memorised the Quran in high school and also mastered the Ten Canonical Recitations. He studied Arabic grammar, morphology, and rhetoric as well as law with a focus on inheritance issues, hadith, and tafsir in Jordan and Yemen.

As a sought-after authority in the Arabic language and tafsir, he has dedicated himself to teaching and writing in these fields for three decades. His journey began with his mother's prayers for him to be like his uncle, who was known to be the most righteous in his family.

Despite being a scholar in his own right, he continues to learn and benefit from his teachers.

Dr Sohail Hanif

He is the Chief Executive of the National Zakat Foundation. He was previously a Lecturer at Cambridge Muslim College and Head of Sciences at Qasid Arabic Institute in Amman. He studied extensively with traditional scholars, including the aforementioned Sheikh Ali Hani, and holds a PhD from Oxford University. His PhD thesis, which explores Islamic legal epistemology, won the 2019 prize of the British Association for Islamic Studies. He has lectured widely on Islamic law and Qur'anic studies in academic, public and traditional settings. He is known for a teaching style that encourages thoughtful inquiry.

MforMoon Illustrations

MforMoon is a freelance illustrator and animator from the UK.

Her work is a unique and exquisite way of combining recitation, story, meaning, image, movement, sound and colour. As well as helping children engage with the stories and wisdom of the Qur'an, each piece of art is also a prayer, a reflection and a joy for adults as well - a way to take a little time out from the stresses of the day and consider Qur'anic verses in a different light.

"The Quran is filled with the most sublime imagery, which most people miss because of a disconnection with Arabic. It is such a bountiful and exquisite language, and sadly most of us lack the linguistic skill to absorb all of its richness," she writes. "I am trying to create a link that helps the listener of the Arabic recitation feel into the realities it expresses."

MforMoon is also a homeschooling mother who has really struggled to find beautifully written and well-researched living books inspired by the Holy Qur'an and the Prophets. Discovering the works of Maryam Sinclair was the answer to a dua she made to fill a crucial gap in her child's education. She writes, "Being invited to illustrate this book has been a true honour and dream come true."

Na'eel Cajee

Born in the United States to immigrant parents from apartheid-era South Africa, Na'eel Cajee is a hafidh with a license in the 10 qira'at and has served as an imam. Currently pursuing advanced studies in the Islamic sciences, Na'eel is also completing his calligraphy apprenticeship in the Ottoman tradition and serves on the board of the Deen Arts Foundation. Na'eel has also spent 12 years at Harvard University, completing bachelors, masters and doctoral degrees in the History of Science, Theological Studies, Dental Medicine, and Endodontics. His Harvard thesis — for which he earned a Summa Cum Laude distinction — focused on responses to epidemics during the French occupation of Egypt (1798-1801). He enjoys honey, historical fiction, and hiking. He lives in Istanbul with his wife and two children.

Mehded Maryam Sinclair, M.Ed.

As an award-winning author and storyteller, Maryam has captured hearts worldwide with her inspiring books and beloved audio productions, acclaimed for their ability to inspire love and solidify Islamic identity in both children and adults.

A revert for nearly 40 years, Maryam's passion lies in uncovering the hidden treasures of the Arabic language in the Qur'an. With the help and expertise of generous scholars of Arabic, Qur'anic interpretation, and history, and gratefully accepting their validations, she has mastered the art of making traditional materials captivating for both young and old.

As a grandmother of seven, at the age of nearly 77, she remains enthusiastic about her continuing study of Arabic and Qur'an. With this beautifully illustrated and adorned book on the life of the Prophet Yusuf, peace upon him, she entices Allah's beloveds to perceive the dazzling miracles of our lives and our deen.